Small Pets

Rabbits

Small Pets

Rabbits

by Vana Haggerty

W. Foulsham & Co. Ltd.
London · New York · Toronto · Cape Town · Sydney

PUBLISHED for Petcetera Press,
235 West First Street,
Bayonne, N.J. 07002. by
W. Foulsham & Company Limited
Yeovil Road, Slough, Berkshire, SL1 4JH

ISBN 0-572-01349-3

Photoset in Great Britain by Filmtype Services
Limited, Scarborough, North Yorkshire and
printed in Spain by Cayfosa. Barcelona.
Dep. Leg. B-33252-1985

Contents

1 The Decision

So you think you would like to keep a rabbit? Have you thought what this involves? Keeping a pet is a responsibility as it has to be fed and watered every day and cleaned out once a week. If you go on holiday somebody has to be found who is willing to do this for you. Good housing for the rabbit is essential, and this costs money, as does buying the equipment you need such as water containers and food bowls.

But you will be greatly rewarded, if you decide to keep a rabbit, by the pleasure you will get from it. The advantages are that you will have a healthy, friendly pet which is also silent – an advantage in some areas – and it can turn into an interesting hobby if you go to rabbit shows and meet people with similar interests.

English Lop
Front cover: French Lop

2 **Housing a Rabbit**

Before you buy your rabbit it is advisable to get everything ready so that when you bring a new rabbit home you can put it straight into a hutch and let it settle down.

Decide the size of rabbit you want, as they range from 900 grams (2 lb) from the smallest dwarf to over 8 kg (18 lb) for the biggest British Giant. This size of the hutch obviously depends on which rabbit you choose. The bigger the hutch you can provide, the better it will be for the rabbit, as they are active animals and there is nothing worse than seeing a rabbit hunched up in a cage which is too small. For an average rabbit the cage size should be 120 cm (4 ft) long by 60 cm (2 ft) high and 90 cm (3 ft) deep. The height is important as rabbits do like to sit up and many shop-made cages are far too low.

The roof, if the cage is to be kept outside, should be sloping backwards with an overhang so that any water runs off, and it should be covered with a waterproof material such as roofing felt, linoleum or thick polythene.

The hutch should be divided into two compartments, one larger than the other. The smaller of the two is for the bedding and should have a solid wooden door. The other, for the rabbit's day area, should be covered in a good strong wire. The better the wire you can put on here, the longer it will last, as rabbits can soon bite holes in flimsy chicken wire. There should be a large enough hole between the two compartments for an adult rabbit to pass through easily. If the gap is too small, rabbits can easily damage their back legs or spines by pushing their way through.

In front of the cage there should be a litter board about 10 cm (4 ins) high to keep in all the woodshavings and straw when you open up the cage. It also prevents a draught blowing in on the rabbit.

It is most important that you have a good catch on the doors. If not, the rabbit will soon be out and you will lose it, or it may be killed by a passing dog or cat. There are several types of catch on the market. If you are handy you can make catches using strips of wood which twist round and keep cage fronts on. These are best for cage fronts which lift right off.

If you are going to have doors with hinges, make sure you buy strong galvanised ones as other types will rust.

This hutch is for a single pet rabbit. If you are more adventurous and keep a few rabbits you can have the hutches in tiers of three or four, or even in blocks of six or eight. These are very space saving although if you buy them they can be expensive.

Most single cages and blocks of cages are made of wood and some blocks of cages have wire floors with galvanised trays under them which catch the droppings. These are easily cleaned out and no wood shavings are necessary.

Morant or ark hutches are hutches with an

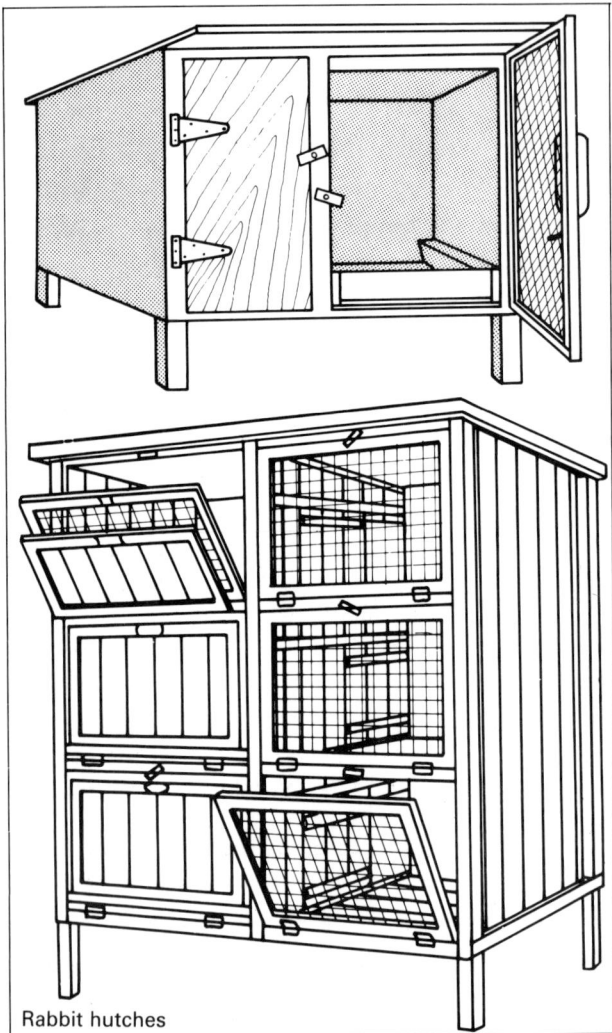

Rabbit hutches

open base which are left on the ground. These
can be moved to fresh grazing every few days
and are ideal if you have plenty of land and are

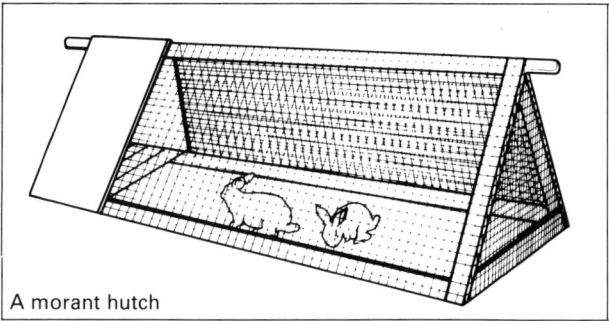
A morant hutch

not feeding the rabbits on pellets. But the rabbits are more at risk from disease and they do have to be carefully looked after, as if the grass is frozen or wet it can cause a lot of stomach troubles.

Commercial rabbitries use wire cages made of 14 gauge wire, 90 cm (3 ft) long by 60 cm (2 ft) wide and suspended from the ceiling of sheds with automatic drinkers and food hoppers all aimed at the minimum amount of labour as they do not have to be cleaned out, the droppings falling into pits below the cages. These wire cages are not suitable for the amateur, as rabbits kept in these conditions have to be in a controlled environment, and they are not suitable for outside use.

If you cannot make a hutch yourself or afford to buy one, a large packing case can be used, with a wire top – this is not the best of cages but if it is a large commercial crate the rabbit will live quite happily in it. The disadvantages are that the rabbit cannot see out and it is hard to clean. It must also be under cover.

All cages must be at least 45 cm (18 ins) off

the ground and at a good height for you to feed and clean out, as if the cage is situated too low you will have to bend all the time, and other animals such as dogs and cats can look in too easily. If the cage is too high, as sometimes happens when you have tiered cages, the rabbit in the top cage is difficult to see or to get out.

If you have a garden it is nice to have a wire run, so that on pleasant days you can put your rabbit out on the lawn for exercise, but remember, always provide a bowl of clean water and some shade, for although rabbits like the sun they do not like too much, and can suffer from heat stroke if left out all day without shelter.

A 2-tier rabbit cage

3 Equipment

Equipment you need for your hutch includes a drinking utensil, food bowl and hay rack.

There are several ways of supplying water to your rabbit and the usual method is by a drinking bottle which you can buy at any pet supplier. These have a screw top with a nozzle fitted. The only disadvantage is that if they are glass they may fall off and break, and the tops never seem to fit other bottles.

The best drinker is a galvanised holder, which is a standard animal drinker, in which you can stand your own bottle such as a plastic lemonade bottle. These drinkers are easy to clean and last for years. You can buy a nozzle separately, the best ones are the ones which have a ball bearing in – these come with a bung and can also be put in your own bottles.

Many people use a pot or bowl for water. If you do this make sure it is heavy so the rabbit cannot tip it over. Usually an earthernware dog bowl is good but you will find that it is often full of wood shavings as rabbits often turn over their bedding.

For food it is best to have a container which is attached to the side or front of the cage, as most rabbits will tip their food over and there will be a lot of waste. The best method is to have a hopper; these are usually made of metal and there are several different types on the market. They can be filled from the outside of

A bottle drinker which takes ordinary lemonade bottles

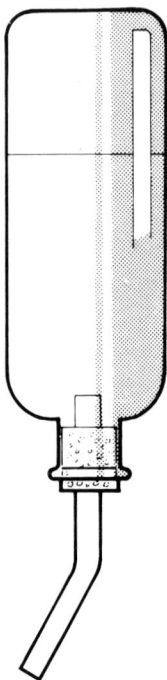

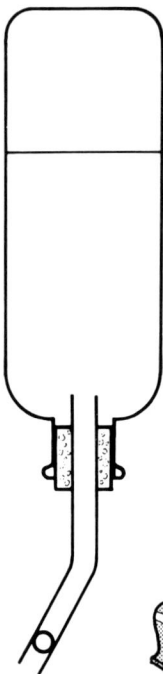

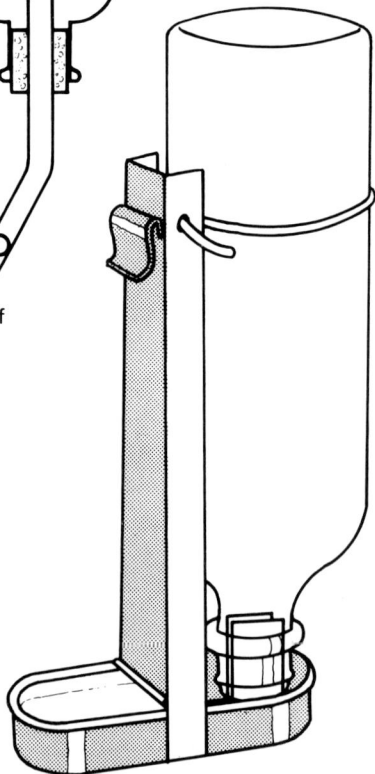

Two different types of drinking bottle

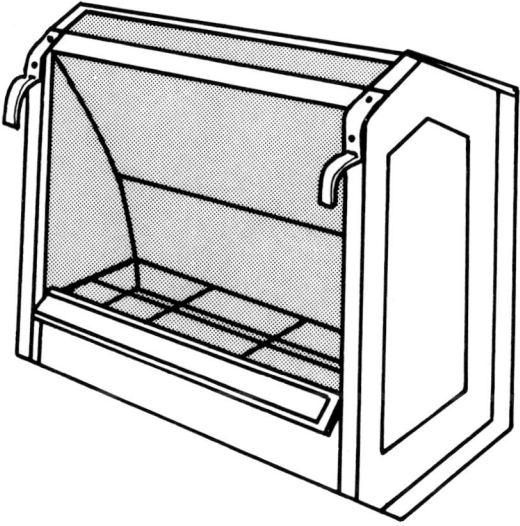

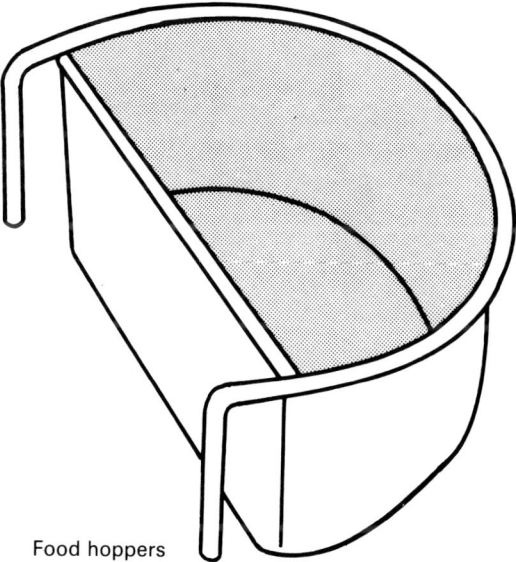

Food hoppers

A rabbit bowl

the cage which saves time. If you use a bowl or pot, make sure it has a very heavy base and is not too big, as some rabbits will use them as toilets.

As your rabbit needs hay it is advisable to have a small hay rack made of wire in the cage, as this saves the rabbit treading on the hay and fouling it.

A scraper or shovel is necessary for cleaning out the cage, and a broom to sweep up. This is all the basic equipment you will need – so now this is all sorted out it is time to choose the breed of rabbit you want to keep.

4 **Selecting the Breed**

Most people are unaware of how many breeds of rabbits there are to choose from – there is, I think, a rabbit to suit everyone – but the rabbits most people see are the cross-bred rabbits usually obtained in a pet shop. These are very pretty and come in all shades and colours, can grow to all sizes, are usually hardy and friendly – but they are like buying a mongrel dog – you don't know how they are going to turn out.

If you want something special to suit you, then there are over 50 breeds of pedigree rabbit to choose from. The following information will help you identify a few breeds, but the best place to see them all is at a rabbit show.

The Netherland Dwarf

One of the smallest and most popular breeds is the Netherland Dwarf. This rabbit weighs at most only just over 1 kg (2½ lb) as an adult and comes in many colours, such as red-eyed whites, black, blue; shaded colours such as sable, smoke pearl, seal point; and tan patterned such as fox, sable martin, and otter. If handled a lot they become very tame.

The advantage of this breed is that they eat very little and it is recommended by Netherland Dwarf breeders that they do not have any greenstuff at all – just rabbit pellets and the occasional carrot. Because of their small ap-

petite their cages do not need to be cleaned out so often, which saves money in woodshavings and straw.

The Polish

The Polish is another small rabbit and is a slimmer version of the Netherland Dwarf. It weighs about 900 grams (2 lb) and is a very neat rabbit which comes in the same colours as the Netherland Dwarfs. It is rarer, however, so if you wanted to obtain one you would have to go to a specialist. These rabbits do not make the best pets, however, as they can have a fiery temperament.

The Dutch

The Dutch is a real favourite for a pet. A very popular, hardy breed which comes in seven colours. Black and white is the most common, but other colours such as chocolate, blue, yellow, tortoise-shell, brown-grey and steel can be found if you want something different. The bucks are smart rabbits with lots of character and will make a better pet, as the does need to be bred from, and if not allowed to breed can become spiteful. Does also have false pregnancies and pull all their fur out to make the nest. Many people find that when their rabbit reaches six months its character changes and they do not realise that it is because it has reached adulthood and is ready to mate.

Dutch rabbits are big eaters for their size and you have to be careful not to overfeed them.

Netherland dwarf

Dutch rabbits showing various colours

The Tan, Himalayan and Californian

The next size of rabbits are breeds such as the Tan, which comes in four colours – black, blue, lilac and chocolate, and the Himalayan which is a slender rabbit with markings like a Siamese cat. It has a docile nature so is good with children. It should not be confused with the Californian which has the same markings but is a much larger rabbit, whose nature is also quiet and contented.

The English and Other Medium-sized Breeds

The English breed of rabbit has a placid temperament and is attractive to look at with its 'butterfly' marked nose and black spots and a stripe down its back. It is one of the oldest fancy breeds of rabbit and makes a very good foster mother as it is very maternal.

Other rabbits of this size are the Silver Fox, the Harlequin Siberians, Havanas and the Chinchilla and many more all weighing from 2.25 kg (5 lb) to 3.6 kg (8 lb).

The Beveren

Larger breeds start with Beverens, which can be coloured in blue, brown, lilac or white. They have a reputation for being a bit spiteful, so although they are lovely to look at they are not really suitable for children.

The New Zealand White and Other Large Breeds

Most people have seen the big white rabbits, albinos with red eyes. These are usually New Zealand Whites. There is a special strain of these called Commercial Whites which are used in commercial rabbit farms. They produce large litters every eight weeks and are very contented rabbits. They can make good pets.

Large breeds like the Chinchilla Giganta, a grey rabbit, and the Flemish Giant, a very quiet rabbit with a long body, have become rarer for two reasons. Firstly commercial breeders don't use them any more as they take longer to grow, and in the rabbit shows the recent arrival of the British Giant, which is the largest of all rabbits, has taken over.

British Giant

The British Giant

The British Giant can weigh anything up to 8 kg (18 lb) or over and has a lovely friendly nature, very large ears and thick fur. The most common colour is Agouti, wild rabbit colour, but you can get steel, black, and white strains. These can have blue or red eyes. They do not like to be picked up, so unless you are good at handling rabbits it is wiser not to have one.

Rex Coated Rabbits

These are just a few breeds – there is a whole section of rabbits called Rex coated rabbits. Their coats are like velvet, very short and dense. People always fall in love with these

Otter rex

when they first see them, but although they look so beautiful there are certain disadvantages to owning one. Mainly they get sore hocks (the underside of their feet) which only have a thin layer of fur rather than a thick carpet slipper like other breeds. The Rex has to be kept on a thick layer of wood shavings and cannot run freely round the garden as they develop large bare patches which often become raw and septic if not treated. The different colours in this breed are well worth looking at if you go to a rabbit show.

The French Lop and the Dwarf French Lop

The French Lop is a rabbit which has become very popular as a pet in recent years. This rabbit's ears lay against its head, hanging down instead of standing up, and it looks like a teddy bear. They are large, powerful rabbits, however, and know their own minds. They weigh up to 5.5 kg (12 lb) and over and make lovely pets if you are lucky enough to get a good natured one, but if by misfortune you get a bad tempered one they are very hard to control. They are also very untidy rabbits and insist on re-arranging the contents of their hutches, banging their food bowls against the side of the cage, and if you have a buck and he can hear other rabbits he will bang his back feet on the hutch floor making a loud noise. The Dwarf French Lop, a smaller version, weighs up to around 2.25 kg (5 lb) and makes a better pet because of its size.

Dalmation rex

French Lop

The English Lop

One of the oldest breeds is also a lop eared rabbit, the English Lop. This rabbit is not suitable for a child as it has very long ears (up to 70 cm (27 ins) from tip to tip) which trail on the floor and are easily damaged.

English Lop

The Angora

The Angora is also not to be recommended. This rabbit weighs 2.7 kg (6 lb) and has wool rather than fur so requires a lot of daily grooming to keep it in good condition. It needs far more time spent on it than most people are willing to spare. Also it is best kept on a wire floor so that its fur does not get matted or fouled.

Angora

5 Buying a Rabbit

People usually buy a rabbit at a pet shop, which generally keep crossbred rabbits from an unknown source. The only problem with this is that you cannot tell how a rabbit will turn out. Will it stay small or grow into an enormous adult? The risk of disease can also be higher, as stock from various places are often mixed together. However, if the rabbit you choose looks healthy and it is what you want, then it is a good place to buy a pet.

If you are after a pedigree rabbit which is a bit more special, then you must find a local rabbit breeder who can either supply you or advise you where to buy the breed you are after. A breeder will know the dates of the local show, where you will be able to look round at all the variety of breeds and get as much advice as you want. These shows are held in most districts every few months and are well worth a visit. Here the breeders sell off their excess stock and young pedigree rabbits can be obtained at a reasonable price.

If you have some difficulty finding your local Rabbit Club write direct to the British Rabbit Council (which is the governing body for Rabbit Breeders) at Purefoy House, 7 Kirkgate, Newark, Nottinghamshire.

What to Look For

When you think you have found the rabbit you want, take a good look at it and check out several things.

1. Is it the sex you want – a buck or a doe?
2. Does it look alert and healthy with bright eyes, a firm back and a sleek coat or, if it is a baby rabbit, a nice fluffy coat?
3. Check the teeth, they should not be overgrown.
4. If the rabbit has a discharge from its nose, eyes or its vent, it is best left and another one chosen.
5. Look in the ears to see that they are clean and that there is no canker, which is a brown discharge caused by mites.
6. Don't forget to ask the person who is selling you the rabbit what it has been used to eating and any other questions you would like answered.

When you at last get your rabbit home, put him into the hutch which has been prepared with wood shavings and straw. Give the rabbit plenty of time to settle down and avoid too much handling at first. Let him get used to you and he will soon become friendly.

Healthy rabbit

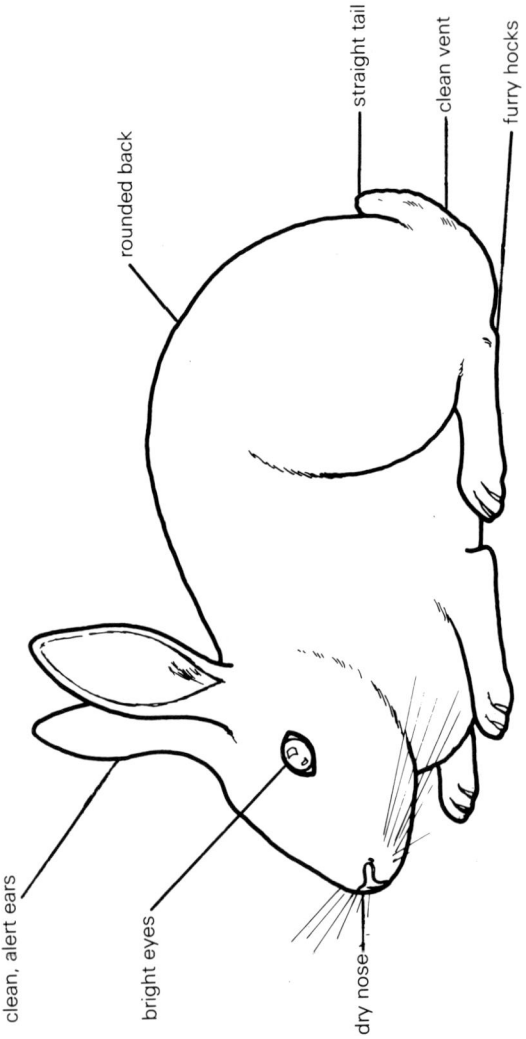

clean, alert ears

bright eyes

dry nose

rounded back

straight tail

clean vent

furry hocks

Unhealthy rabbit

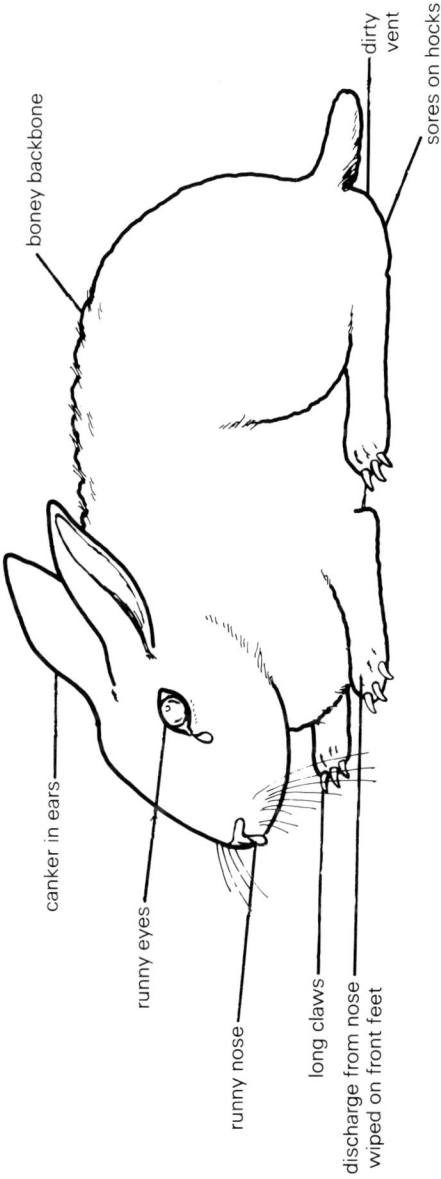

boney backbone

dirty
vent

sores on hocks

canker in ears

runny eyes

runny nose

long claws

discharge from nose
wiped on front feet

6 **Food and Water**

Rabbit Pellets

Most rabbits today are fed on pellets, which are small green or brown pellets about 12 mm (½ inch) long and up to 5 mm (¼ inch) wide. They contain everything a rabbit needs to keep healthy and fit, including all the minerals and vitamins. In fact, they are a complete meal. They also contain coccidiostats which is a drug which reduces the odds of rabbit catching coccidiosis, a disease of the liver and bowel wall.

Because of the difference in diet, rabbits and cavies should not be kept in the same hutch. Cavies need a food pellet which is ACS (anti coccidiostat) free as if they eat the rabbit pellets the natural bacterias in the cavies' stomach are killed and the animal will be undersized. They also need vitamin C which is given in their water. Apart from diet, it is not advisable to keep them together as a rabbit will mount a cavy causing it some distress and often biting it between the ears at the back of the neck, and a buck rabbit can cause damage to a cavy's eyes if it sprays over them.

If fed on pellets, however, rabbits can grow very fat so only the correct amount must be given. This is 85 grams (3 oz) a day for the average size rabbit. Usually a handful in the morning and a handful at night is enough. If the

The contents of a rabbit pellet

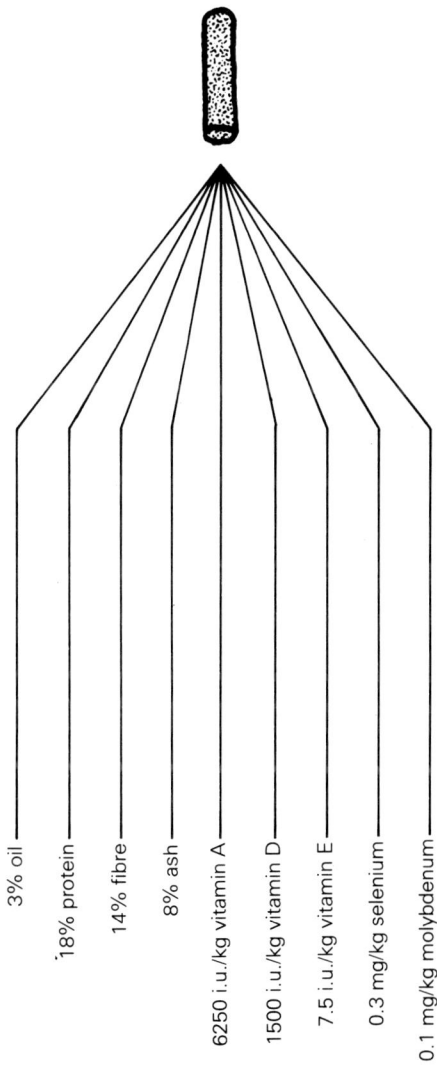

3% oil

18% protein

14% fibre

8% ash

6250 i.u./kg vitamin A

1500 i.u./kg vitamin D

7.5 i.u./kg vitamin E

0.3 mg/kg selenium

0.1 mg/kg molybdenum

rabbit doesn't get much exercise it is no good overfeeding as this can lead to a number of illnesses.

Other Foods

Rabbit mix, which can be obtained from pet shops, is another alternative. This consists of a mixture of cereals such as oats, maize, barley, soya beans and grass meal. It has more variety than pellets and rabbits enjoy it.

Traditionally people have fed rabbits on root crops, green food and stale bread. Root crops such as sugar beet, mangolds and swedes and green food such as cabbage, kale and cauliflower leaves are fine if you can work out the quantity to feed, but make sure all the food is dry and clean before giving it to the animal and be especially careful that no chemical or insecticide has been near it.

Wild foods such as brambles, dandelion leaves, coltsfoot leaves and sow thistle are all very palatable but beware of giving too much. If fed in excess, dandelion leaves can cause the rabbit's urine to turn a bright red colour, and most greens have a laxative effect. The best advice is to feed green foods with caution.

Foods which should never be given are grass cuttings; wild leaves that have been picked where a dog could have fouled on them; bulbous plants such as blue bells, daffodils or any flowers; and rhubarb or uncooked potato peelings.

Bread can be heated in a low oven which hardens it up and is good for the rabbit to chew on.

Hay

Whichever way you feed, it is essential that you include hay in the diet. This is because it contains essential fibre. It also keeps rabbits from being bored as they can sit and nibble all day. Always use sweet meadow hay: it must not smell musty or look damp, as this can do a lot of damage and can even kill a rabbit. The best hay contains wild plants, it should smell fresh and be dust free. Also find hay that is a few months old as newly baled hay is far too rich, and if fed to a rabbit it will scour very badly and could result in the rabbit dying.

Water

Fresh water should be given every day especially if a rabbit is fed on pellets or rabbit mix as these are both very dry. Even if fed on greenstuff, the animals will still get thirsty especially in the summer. Check every morning that your water containers are working as sometimes they become blocked or are at the wrong angle so the water is not getting through and the rabbit is unable to drink.

7 General Management

Take your rabbit out frequently and give it a good inspection. It is only by handling it that you will see that it is well and in good condition. Often rabbits sit in hutches and have scours or long claws that their owners do not notice until the condition is so bad that the rabbit is in a very poor way.

Handling Rabbits

The more you handle your pet the tamer it will become so you must learn the correct way to hold it. If not you will end up being scratched, which will put you off picking up rabbits, and the rabbit will feel insecure and frightened.

The full weight of the rabbit should be supported by one hand on its hindquarters while the other hand holds the back of the rabbit's neck. It should be held away from you and facing you. This is how judges hold them at shows so that at a glance they can inspect the rabbit. If you can learn to do this while the rabbit is young, by the time it is an adult it will lie quite still when you pick it up. Some rabbits are so heavy that it is difficult for a child to pick them up in the correct way. However, as long as the rabbit is comfortable and its weight is supported, it will not struggle.

Holding a rabbit correctly

When removing a rabbit from its hutch bring it out backwards so that its feet do not drag and it does not catch its hind legs on the doors. They are much easier to get out this way especially if the opening is small.

Trimming the Claws

The claws of a rabbit will wear down naturally if it gets a lot of exercise, however, as most of them sit in a hutch all day their claws will need trimming every so often. In a white rabbit which has white toe nails it is easy to see where to cut them (about 6 mm (¼ inch) below the quick), but in black and coloured rabbits you have to be far more careful as you cannot see where the vein ends, so just trim off the points or if they are very long, use your discretion. If you do cut them too short and they bleed, do not worry as they soon heal up.

With small breeds you can use nail clippers, but for larger breeds a special nail cutter is required. If you do not feel you cut them correctly a rabbit breeder will always help you. Alternatively take your rabbit to a vet and watch how he does it.

Grooming and Moulting

Rabbits groom themselves and one in good healthy condition should keep itself clean. But a good brush, especially when they are moult-

Cutting a rabbit's claws

The correct way to clip the claws

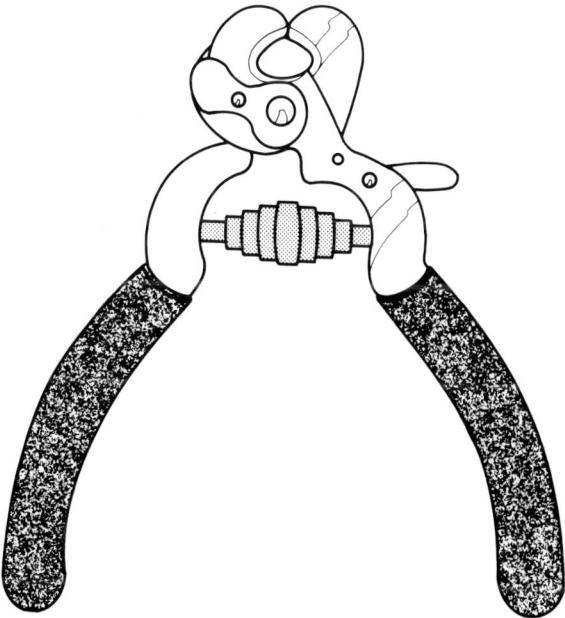

Claw clippers

Holding pet rabbits

ing, helps to get rid of loose hair. Just stroking your hand over a rabbit will help its coat become shiny.

Rabbits moult several times a year, depending on the temperature, and bucks in particular can become very run down if the moult con-

tinues for too long and they often go off their food. Rabbits lose their first coat at about four months of age depending on the breed. This is when their baby coat comes out, as the adult coat is growing underneath.

8 **Cleaning Out**

It is very important that the rabbit's cage should be kept as clean as possible. This means cleaning out at least once a week. If you are lucky and have a tidy rabbit who only goes to the toilet in one corner of the hutch, it will not be necessary to take all the wood shavings and straw out. You can put a small tray of earth in the corner, such as a seed tray, and your rabbit will become trained to use it. All you have to do is to remove the tray and refill with fresh earth or wood shaving.

Every month the cage should be scrubbed clean as this will stop any diseases developing. Use hot water with a detergent or five per cent solution of washing soda. Then rewash with clean water and a disinfectant. Really get into the corners of the cage with a scrubbing brush, and do not forget to do the wire which gets full of dust and fur. Let the cage dry in the sun if possible, sprinkle some lime on the hutch floor to keep it smelling sweet before you put on clean bedding.

If you are going to use a second-hand hutch for your new pet you must creosote it after scrubbing it thoroughly. This will make doubly sure that no disease is lingering, but test it to see that the creosote has dried and its does not smell too strong before you put the rabbit back into the hutch. This is because the creosote fumes will affect the rabbit's eyes and make its life very unpleasant.

Apart from cleaning the cage, all the food containers should be cleaned as often as possible. If dust or old food are left in them it will be no good for your rabbit's health. Make sure that water containers are not green inside. The best way to clean bottles is to add rock salt, uncooked rice or shredded newspaper with some water and shake the bottle up and down.

If you have wire cages they obviously do not need to be cleaned out as often, as all the droppings fall through the wire floor, but these do need completely scrubbing every few months as rabbit fur builds up on the wire and it becomes very dusty. It it is very bad, a blow torch can burn the fur off the wires and then the whole cage can be thoroughly cleaned. Put the rabbit some distance away when you do this as particles of dust travel through the air and it will make your rabbit sneeze if it breathes in the dust.

If you keep the hutch clean you will not attract flies which carry disease and it is likely your rabbit will live longer and certainly be happier – many problems such as runny eyes are caused simply by ammonia fumes from their droppings. The rule is: if you can smell a rabbit, it needs cleaning out.

9 Illnesses and Diseases

If you keep your rabbit clean and well fed and its hutch well maintained, it is doubtful if your pet will catch any of these diseases. But however careful you are, there is a time when rabbits catch something or other. It is wise to know if the condition is serious and you need to consult a vet, or if you can deal with it yourself. Rabbits die very easily, however, and unless the pet is especially valuable it is not worth paying a lot of money at a vet when often it dies anyway.

Scours or Enteritis

Enteritis, or scours as most rabbit breeders call it, is one of the most common complaints rabbits are particularly prone to at about eight weeks of age. This is when the rabbit's droppings become very loose and it sits huddled up in the corner of the cage looking very dejected. The rabbit's hindquarters get very soiled, and if not treated it will soon die.

The main reason for this is that it has eaten something alien or its diet has been changed suddenly – too many wet or dry greens, mouldy root crops, too fresh hay or any food that has been contaminated either by the rabbit fouling the food itself or by mice or rats.

Often nothing can be done, but if you notice it soon enough you can try putting indigestion powder in the drinking water to settle the stomach and removing any food that looks as if it could have caused the trouble. Also you can try strawberry, bramble, raspberry or shepherd's purse leaves. Often you can tempt a rabbit to eat these if it is off its normal food.

Coccidiosis

Most owners with pet rabbits have never heard of this ailment and yet it is very common. It is caused by a small parasite called coccidia, carried by most rabbits. The symptoms are usually to be seen as a pot belly – the rabbit looks very bloated due to the disease affecting the liver or intestines. Often a rabbit will just be found dead in its cage. If it does survive it will be very slow to grow and remain in poor condition.

There are two different types of coccidiosis. The one which is not always fatal attacks the liver. The other form is found in the intestinal walls. The rabbit again looks in poor condition with a harsh coat and eats twice as much as normal without putting on any weight. This is because the rabbit is not absorbing any nourishment due to the coccidea in the intestines.

A drug can be administered, such as Sulphaquinoxaline which is available from the vet, and this often cures the disease if it can be caught sufficiently early, but it is rarely worth keeping a rabbit with bad coccidiosis.

If you are putting a rabbit into a cage which has been contaminated by a rabbit with this disease it must be properly cleaned with plenty of disinfectant and left empty for as long as possible. This is because the life cycle of a coccidia is such that is can soon contaminate another rabbit. If you put your rabbit out on the grass in its wire run, move it to a different area so that the rabbit is not eating infected grass.

The main way of combating coccidiosis is by feeding with rabbit pellets which contain a drug called coccidostats. This is added to the pellets when they are manufactured and it immunises the rabbit against the disease.

Malocclusion of Teeth

One more reason why a rabbit might be losing weight is the fact that its teeth do not meet. Normally the rabbit's upper and lower incisors touch and grind down as they eat. If they do not meet correctly, they continue to grow and

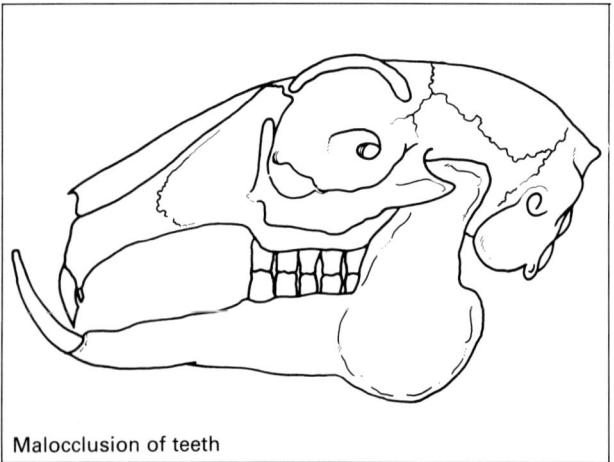

Malocclusion of teeth

the rabbit becomes unable to eat – eventually dying from starvation.

This is usually a hereditary trait in some strains, but it can be caused by a rabbit damaging its teeth by pulling at the wire of its cage.

It is a good idea to put a block of wood in the cage – it can be screwed to the side of the hutch where the rabbit can chew it. Holly wood is excellent as it is very hard. It will save the edges of your cages and litter boards from being eaten.

There is no cure for malocclusion although you can try cutting the teeth down. This is often distressing for the rabbit, although it does sometimes work. As often as not, however, they regrow again, so the best advice is to have the rabbit destroyed. Do not breed from a rabbit with this complaint as it will come out in its offspring.

Bloat

This is when the rabbit looks full of air, and when held its stomach feels full of gas. This is because gas forms in the caecum and usually makes a sound like fluid slopping around. The cause of this is usually eating too much fresh food such as grass, clover or fresh hay. The rabbit looks very unhappy and will sit very still with its eyes glazed and often grinding its teeth. If it is a young rabbit it will most probably die. There is not much you can do except keep it warm and give an indigestion powder in the water. Make sure any greenstuff is removed.

Pneumonia

A rabbit often dies of pneumonia after it has had some other disease and its resistance is low. Pneumonia is an inflammation of the lungs and often occurs if the rabbit is in a draught or is sitting in damp conditions. The only way to diagnose this condition is that the rabbit's breathing is very rapid, it looks miserable and huddled up, and loses its appetite. Sometimes a rabbit's eyes will glaze over or a discharge will come out of the corners of the eyes.

Keep the rabbit warm with plenty of bedding, but allow fresh air to circulate. Do not keep it indoors or in a stuffy shed.

Snuffles and Sneezing

Snuffles is the disease that rabbit breeders dread. It starts off with the rabbit sneezing – at first it could be dust or something irritating the rabbit's nose. If, it continues, however, and a thick, whitish-yellow discharge is seen coming from the nostrils, then the odds are your rabbit has contracted snuffles.

At first the rabbit will not look too bad and its appetite will stay the same. But as the condition worsens, the front legs get very matted where they wipe their noses on them and sneezing becomes more and more continuous.

This disease of the lungs is caused by a bacteria of the pasteurella group. One type of pasteurella is called Bordetella bronchiseptica. When affected by this, the rabbit seems almost normal but its fur under its nose is always moist.

If you just have one pet rabbit, snuffles is not disastrous but if you have more than one, the sick rabbit must be isolated at once. As the disease is air-borne, the sick rabbit must be a long way from any others.

Antibiotics can be obtained from the vet, but although all the symptoms can disappear a rabbit can carry snuffles and pass it on to others. If you keep a lot of rabbits do not breed from any you suspect are carriers and it is best if they are culled.

Colds

Rabbits can catch colds if kept in bad conditions. It must not be confused with snuffles as both ailments have a discharge from the nose. With a cold it is more likely to be a clear fluid. The rabbit may also have runny eyes. Remove the rabbit away from any draughts, keep it warm, and if the discharge from its nose is bad, clean it up with a solution of ten per cent boracic acid.

Canker

If a rabbit constantly shakes its head or scratches its ears with its hind legs, it has probably got canker. This is a very small mite which gets right inside the ear and causes inflammation. A crusty substance builds up, gradually blocking the whole ear. It is easily identified as it is a yellow-brown colour. When you find the rabbit has got this do not try and poke it out with cotton wool sticks as you can push it down further onto the rabbit's eardrum.

There are lots of treatments sold in shops for similar conditions in cats. These parasiticide drops are very effective and a few drops night and morning for a few days, or as advised on the packet, will soon clear it up. It is most important to clean the rabbit's hutch out so that if there are any mites left they will be destroyed and the rabbit will not be re-infected.

Mange is also caused by mites but these affect the skin and red patches appear when the rabbit scratches itself. This is not very common but a vet can soon give you something to cure it.

Myxomatosis

Myxomatosis was the main killer of rabbits after the germ was introduced by farmers in 1953 to keep the population of wild rabbits under control. Every now and then there is still an outbreak, and if a mosquito or a flea from a rabbit which is carrying myxomatosis comes into contact with your pet rabbit it can contaminate it. This can happen if people take their dog for a walk in an affected area – the dog then plays with the pet and the disease is passed on.

A rabbit suffering from this disease is a horrible sight. If you live in an area where there is known to be myxomatosis have your rabbit vaccinated. There is no known cure, so directly myxomatosis is diagnosed the rabbit must be culled.

Sore hocks

Not many people look enough at their rabbit's feet. The hocks are the undersides of the rear feet and should have a thick coating of fur which keeps the rabbit warm. However, some rabbits, particularly Rex breeds, have very thin fur and soon have sore bald spots appearing. These then break and become septic and the rabbit suffers considerable discomfort. It can also be caused if rabbits are kept on uneven wire floors which wears the fur away. The cure for this is to keep the rabbit on a thick pile of bedding. Treat the sore place with a zinc ointment and keep it clean.

Worms and Fleas

Rabbits very rarely get worms. Occasionally they get thread worms which look like a small piece of white cotton about 6 mm (¼ inch) long. They come from the small intestines and pass out when the rabbit goes to the toilet. If the rabbit gets heavily infested it can be treated by a worm powder obtainable from the vet. A rabbit can catch tapeworms if it is allowed in an area where the droppings of a cat or dog have been. The eggs of the tape worm are passed out onto the grass and the rabbit can become infected if it eats the grass. The rabbit can be treated with a worm powder.

Fleas are very rare on rabbits but must be dealt with at once. Apart from making the rabbit scratch they might contain myxomatosis. Dust the rabbit with flea powder being careful not to get any in its eyes. Follow the instructions carefully and brush out all the powder.

10 Sexing and Mating Rabbits

What you must know if you decide to breed rabbits is how to sex them. It is surprising how many people never look to see what sex their rabbit is and are often keeping a rabbit which is a doe when they bought it thinking it was a buck or vice versa.

When they are adult you can see at a glance: the buck, or male rabbit, has two testicles one either side of his reproductive organ. When the rabbit is under 20 weeks, you will have to hold the rabbit and press gently with your index finger and thumb on either side of the reproductive organ. By doing this you will see if the organ is a rounded protrusion, which means it's a male, or a V-shaped slit which is pointed at one end, which means it is a doe.

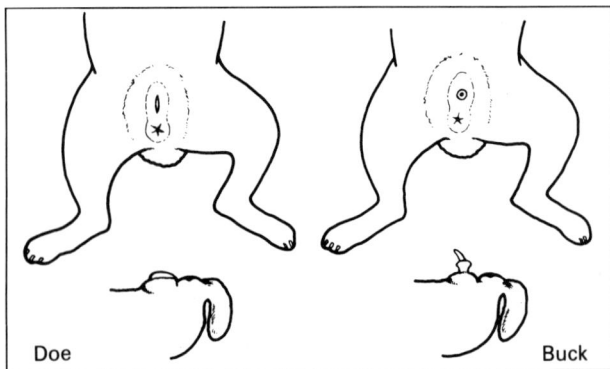

Doe   Buck

Rabbit breeders can sometimes tell by the shape of the head as bucks often have broader heads than does. Another way of telling is by the temperament of the rabbit. Bucks are usually more lively and have a lot of character. If they can smell another rabbit they may spray it with urine – which smells stronger than the doe's urine – so as to attract attention to themselves.

Adult does are usually more contented. They tend to over-eat if allowed to and will get very fat if not bred. Sometimes a doe can get very spiteful and often owners are frightened to put their hands in the cage. This is because they want mating. Usually they calm down again or start making high nests of fur and guarding them as if they are full of babies; this is called a pseudo-pregnancy. Because all the symptoms are there, the doe becomes fatter, her mammary glands begin to work and pet owners are convinced that the rabbit is about to give birth.

It is unadvisable to keep two rabbits together when they are adult as even two of the same sex will mount each other and often stimulate each other; where one is more dominant it will bite the other rabbit behind its ears. Does can act like bucks and pet owners often think they are just playing games.

If you decide you would like to breed rabbits there are certain considerations to think about. Firstly rabbits can have up to ten babies, which is too many for the average rabbit to rear. Are you prepared to cull half of these? Secondly, will you be able to find homes for them? After a few months you will need separate cages for the babies or they will all be mating with each other. Pet shops do not usually want them, and if they do only offer a small amount. It costs a lot to feed a litter and you can find yourself out of pocket.

The best age to start breeding rabbits is around 22 weeks for a doe and 24 for a buck depending on the breed. You should not attempt to breed from rabbits over a year if they have not bred before. If you do not know how old your rabbit is, it is best to leave them, as older rabbits can develop problems. The same applies to a buck – if he is mated once he will know what he is missing and the excitement can also cause the rabbit to have a heart attack if he is old.

If you have a buck and a doe they should always be kept in separate cages or your doe will be permanently pregnant. The doe will show signs of restlessness when she wants mating, by turning her bedding over or throwing her food container about or by pulling at the wire in the front of the cage.

Take her out and look at her sexual organs, these normally are pale pink, but if they are much redder with a purple tinge then she is on heat and ready to mate. Make sure she is healthy and clean. If you are not sure if she is ready to mate put her in with the buck and you will soon see, as does will not mate if they do not want to.

Check the buck before you put the doe in his cage. Never do it the other way round as the doe is likely to attack the buck and injure him. If both the buck and doe are ready to mate watch very closely as it is over in a second. The doe will lift her back up and the buck will mount her from behind. When he has mated her he will roll over and sometimes squeal. If he has mated properly he will begin to bang his back feet just to let everyone know.

To be doubly sure you can let them mate again if the doe is willing, or remate a few hours later. Do not leave the buck and doe together in the cage as the buck will continue to try and mate until he is exhausted. He will also pull the doe's fur out. Put the doe back in her cage and write the date of mating down on a card and pin it on the side of the cage so that you do not forget when you mated her and when the babies are due so you can prepare her cage.

Rabbits mating

11 Kinderling

Does carry their babies for 31 days – and most rabbits have their litters on the expected day. If they do not and the rabbit seems all right, leave her alone and do not do anything unless she is well overdue and looks fretful.

Do not overfeed her while she is carrying – continue with her normal diet for 14 days and if she seems very hungry you can begin to give her a bit more food towards the end of her pregnancy. During the last week the doe will become much larger and she will lie on her side with her stomach spread out. She will appear very contented.

Some does will begin to make their nests a week or more before they have their young. They collect up any bedding in their mouths and re-arrange it in the corner of the hutch, heaping up wood shavings on top. When you see this happening it is time to put in a nest box. This is not necessary if you have a warm bedding compartment but if the rabbit is in a big cage or wire-floored cage it is essential. The nest box is a wooden box with sides about 15 to 20 cm (6 to 8 ins) high, and 45 cm (18 ins) long and 30 cm (12 ins) wide – enough room for a rabbit to lie down comfortably.

If the doe is seen to be making a nest 17 days after she has been mated she has probably missed. If there is evidence of fur plucked from her body on the floor of the cage at this stage then it can be a pseudo-pregnancy. If this happens the doe will be very fertile and she must be remated at once.

The doe will have the babies on her own and should not need any assistance. The babies are born very quickly, cleaned and tucked up in the nest of fur she has pulled out of her chest. The doe eats the afterbirth and cleans up. Make sure she has plenty of clean drinking water as from now she will drink up to 1½ litres (2¼ pt) a day to provide milk for the babies. Often there will be a dead baby in the litter; this is best removed as soon as possible, but often the doe will eat it so you might not even be aware of it. The usual litter is between six and nine babies. Some litters go up to fourteen and some only have two. The number to aim for is around six as this means there is plenty of milk for them all.

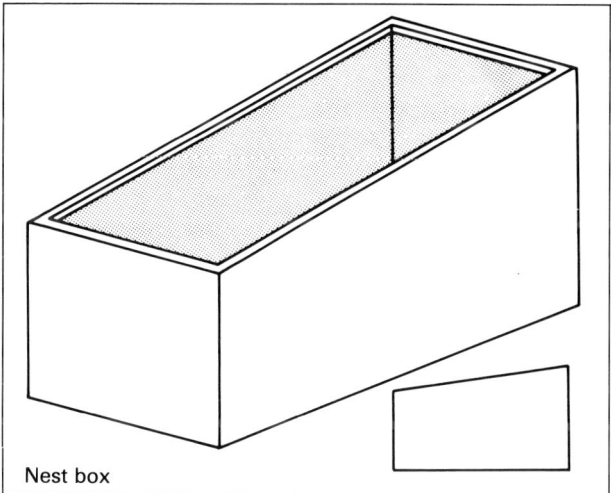

Nest box

When you look in the nest to decide which to take out, distract the doe by giving her something to eat and stroke her before you touch the babies so that your hand smells of her. Do not touch a dog or cat before you do this as if rabbits can smell any other animal on their babies they are likely to kill them. Remove the smallest

Doe and her young in a pen

rabbits or the ones which are mismarked in such breeds at Dutch and English and kill them quickly.

The baby rabbits are born blind and with no fur, although usually you can see what colour they will be by the colour of their skin. The rabbit's milk is very nutritious and the babies

should grow at a fast rate. Within four days they should have the start of a fur coat and should be fat, podgy babies. If they are thin and making any noise, they are hungry and the mother is not feeding them.

There are many reasons for this. She might have mastitis. This is where the teats become inflamed and the milk is not getting through. The milk builds up and becomes like cheese in the doe. This is very sore and it soon becomes septic. Antibiotics can be used and the nipples bathed in warm water to try and start the milk flow. If mastitis occurs the babies do not usually survive – it is not worth hand rearing them unless you have plenty of time and patience and it is often a lost labour as they die anyway. If you decide to feed them yourself, goat's milk is the best substitute for the doe's milk.

The babies open their eyes when they are nine days old but if being fed properly by the mother make no attempt to leave the nest until they are two and a half weeks old.

By the time they are four weeks they should have started to eat on their own and many commercial rabbitries wean their babies at this age. They remate the doe two weeks after her last litter. The doe is very fertile after she has had babies so do not let a buck anywhere near her unless you want another litter.

The best time to remate her is between six or eight weeks after she has had her last litter. Rabbits usually keep healthier if they are allowed to breed, especially if they are fed on a high protein diet.

12 Showing Rabbits

If you are really interested in rabbits, the rabbit show is the place to go. You will notice that rabbits here all wear a metal ring on their hind legs with numbers and letters on. This indicates the year of birth, type and the rabbit's own registration number. For example a Dutch rabbit born in 1983 might read BRC (British Rabbit Council), 83 (the year), B. (type of rabbit), 08586 (the rabbit's registration number).

The other ring numbers are as follows:

Size A   Polish

Size B   Argente Creme, Dutch, Dwarf Lop, Himalayan Tan, Tri-colour Dutch.

Size C   Argente Bleu, Argente Brun.

Size D   Chinchilla, English Lilac Sable, all Foxes, Havannas, Siberian Silvers, Smoke Pearl.

Size E   Angora, Argente, Champagne, Harlequin, New Zealand Red, all Rex strains.

Size G   Beveren Blanc-de-Hotor, Belgian Hare, English Lop.

Size H   Flemish, French Lop, Giant Rabbits, New Zealand White, New Zealand Black, Blanc de Bouscat, Blanc de Termond.

Size L   Chinchilla Giganta, Californian, Alaska, Rhinelander, Thuringer.

Size X   Netherland Dwarf.

All rabbits must wear the correct ring to enter a show unless they are entered into pet classes which are for rabbits of indiscriminate breedings who are judged on their condition and tameness. These metal rings are put on the rabbits when they are about eight weeks old and they just slide over the back foot and position on the joint. Sometimes a rabbit will grow very big and fat and the ring will get tight and grow into the leg of the animal. If your rabbit has been ringed it is wise to check the ring occasionally just to make sure the rabbit is not suffering.

There are other ways of identifying large amounts of rabbits, and in commercial herds they tattoo a number on the rabbit's ear and in other places put a metal tag through the ear.

In England, only rabbits with rings on their legs are acceptable. If you purchase a rabbit with a ring and you are a member of the British Rabbit Club which gives you a membership number then you must get a transfer card from whoever is selling you the rabbit. This should be signed by both you and the seller and sent to the BRC to be registered in your name.

Travelling

If you do decide to show your rabbit regularly you can buy a travelling box for your rabbit. They are made of light wood and have a carrying strap. There is no way your pet can escape, which sometimes happens if you put it in a box.

Entering a Show

If you decide to enter a show you must find out the details in advance as you will have to enter your rabbit usually two or three days before the show – or even two or three weeks if it is a very big show.

There are lots of classes in which your rabbit can be entered and on the day it can be on the judges' table up to eight times if it is very good. The best policy is to ask whoever is running the show to help you decide which classes to enter your rabbit in.

All show rabbits must be booked in on the show day before ten o'clock, or at whatever time stated on the schedule. They will be put in pens with numbers on and throughout the day will be brought out and judged. Each breed will be judged separately and the best of these will be judged against the other breed winners to find the best in the show. This is a day when you can talk to your heart's content about your rabbit and have any queries answered.

I hope after reading this book you still decide that you would like to keep a rabbit and I hope the information you have read will help you to keep a fit, happy and healthy pet.

The full range of
titles in the
LOVE YOUR PET SERIES is:-